ARTOLA

001

002

LAS VEGAS

003

004

Dionnetta

005

006

SCOTT KELTIE

007

008

009

010

011

012

013

014

015

016

017

018

019

020

021

022

023

024

025

026

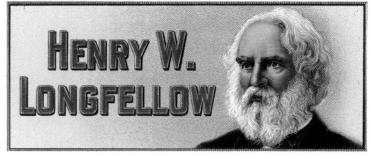

027

028

029

030

031

032

033

034

035

036

037

039

040

GEN.DAYTON

041

042

043

044

045

046

047

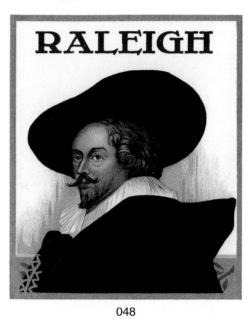

048

049

050

051

052

053

054

055

056

057

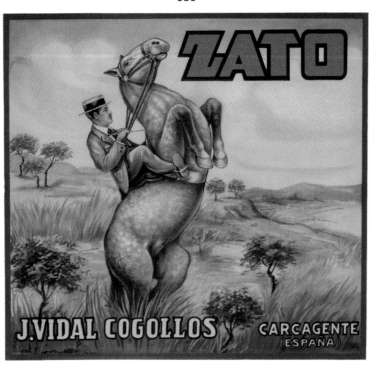

058

059   FRUIT CRATE LABELS   7

060

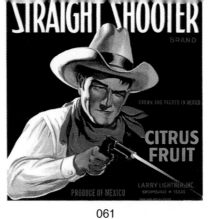

061

062

063

065

066

064

069

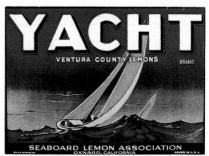

067

073

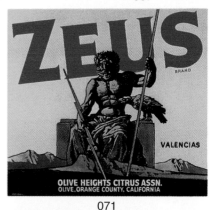

071

074

068

070

072

075

076

077

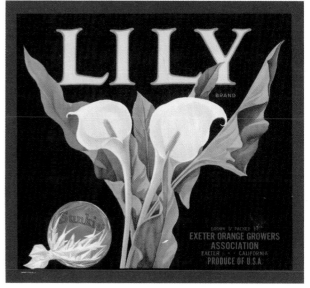

078

079

080

081

082

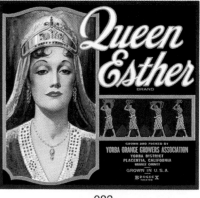

083

084

086

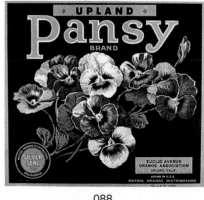

087

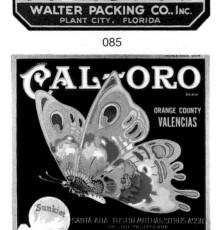

085

090

088

091

089

092

093

094

095

096

097

098

099

CARLTON HÔTEL LUCERNE

100

ANFA-HOTEL CASABLANCA

101

PALACE HOTEL "CIGA HOTELS" MILANO

PIAZZA REPUBBLICA 20 - TELEF. 6336

S. p. A. Richter & C. – Napoli

102

COPACABANA PALACE RIO DE JANEIRO

103

RATSKELLER HOTEL RESTAURANT ROTHENBURG o. T.

104

N.G.Y M/N AVGVSTVS

105

HOTEL COLOMBIA GENOVA

106

TOKYO IMPERIAL HOTEL JAPAN

帝国ホテル

107

HOTEL **MINERVA** FIRENZE

108

DOMINION HÔTEL AVIGNON

109

LAC DE COMO CERNOBBIO

GRAND HOTEL **VILLA d'ESTE**

110

GROSVENOR Park Lane London, W. **HOUSE**

111

WALD-HOTEL
BEI RÜDESHEIM AM RHEIN

JAGDSCHLOSS-NIEDERWALD

112

KYOTO HOTEL
KYOTO JAPAN

113

HOTEL del NOGARO
MONTEVIDEO

114

SCHWEIZERHOF
ZÜRICH

115

HOTEL LUNA
VENEZIA

116

HUSA
GRANADA
HOTEL
ALHAMBRA PALACE

117

JAL
JAPAN AIR LINES
日本航空

118

SEMIRAMIS
CAIRO
HOTEL

119

VICTORIA HOTEL
AMSTERDAM

120

HOTEL BAD SCHACHEN
LINDAU - BODENSEE

121

BATAVIA
JAVA
HOTEL DES INDES

122

123

124

125

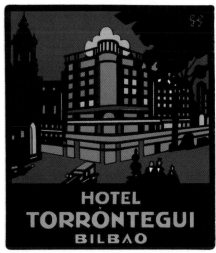

126

127

128

129

130

131

132

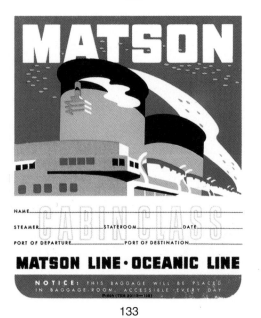

133

134

135

136

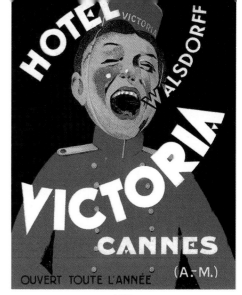

138

139

137

140

141

142

143

144

HONG KONG HOTEL

HONG KONG, CHINA

145

NORDDEUTSCHER LLOYD BREMEN

146

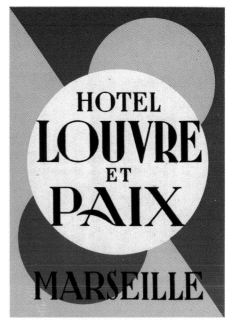

HOTEL LOUVRE ET PAIX

MARSEILLE

147

PALAZZO & AMBASCIATORI

ROMA

148

Hotel Wilden Mann Luzern

149

Hotel CASABLANCA

GRANADA-(ESPAÑA)

150

MARRAKECH

HOTEL DE LA MAMOUNIA

153

GRAZ-AUSTRIA

HOTEL STEIRERHOF

151

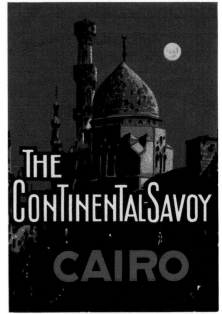

THE CONTINENTAL SAVOY

CAIRO

152

Hotel NEW GRAND YOKOHAMA JAPAN

154

LLOYD SABAUDO 1a Cl. GENOVA Conte Verde

NOME DEL PASSEGGERO

BAGAGLIAIO

155

156

157

158

159

160

161

162

163

164

165

166

167

Lady Marian
TOILET WATER

Salux
Perfumer
St.Louis,
U.S.A.

168

SALKO

Florida Water

SALUX
PERFUMER
St.Louis,
U.S.A.

169

CRÊME GLORIA
A GREASELESS
VANISHING CREAM
FOR THE SKIN.
Dr. J.B. Lynas & Son.
LOGANSPORT,
INDIANA.

170

BUERGER'S
Floral Lilac
TOILET WATER
MANUFACTURED BY
THE BUERGER BROS SUPPLY C?
DENVER, COLO.

171

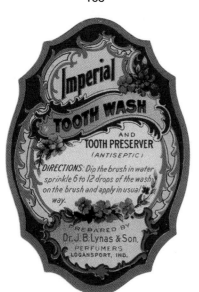

Imperial
TOOTH WASH
AND
TOOTH PRESERVER
(ANTISEPTIC)

DIRECTIONS: Dip the brush in water
sprinkle 6 to 12 drops of the wash
on the brush and apply in usual
way.

PREPARED BY
Dr. J.B. Lynas & Son.
PERFUMERS
LOGANSPORT, IND.

172

Standard
BAY RUM
Contains 37% Grain Alcohol.

GUARANTEED BY PHIL EISEMANN UNDER FOOD &
DRUG ACT, JUNE 30, 1906, SERIAL NO.
34078

Prepared by
PHIL EISEMANN
LANCASTER, PA.

173

Acme
Hair
Vigor
40%
GRAIN
ALCOHOL

An Excellent Preparation
for Dandruff
And
Falling
Hair.

GUARANTEED
BY PHIL EISEMANN
UNDER THE PURE
FOOD & DRUGS ACT
JUNE 30, 1906
SERIAL NO. 34078.

Prepared by
Phil Eisemann
Lancaster,
Pa.

174

SanRemo

Toilet
Water
A
DELIGHTFUL
TOILET REQUISITE

Dr. J.B. Lynas & Son.
Perfumers.
LOGANSPORT.
IND.

175

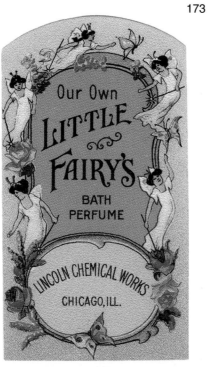

Our Own
LITTLE
FAIRY'S
BATH
PERFUME

LINCOLN CHEMICAL WORKS
CHICAGO, ILL.

176

BUERGER'S
COM-ADE

A Tonic Aid
to
the Better Combing
of Hair

THE BUERGER BROS.
SUPPLY CO.
DENVER

177

IMPORTED

BAY RUM
FOR EXTERNAL USE ONLY
ALCOHOL CONTENTS 50%
BOTTLED BY
PHIL EISEMANN
616 N. QUEEN ST.
LANCASTER, PA.

178

179

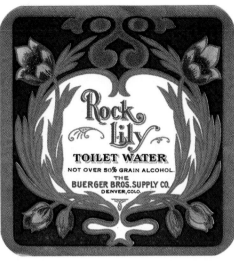

180

COOLING AND SOOTHING FACE LOTION

BUEROMA

THE BUERGER BROS. SUPPLY CO.

DENVER

181

EAU DE COLOGNE SUPÉRIEURE

183

182

184

185

186

187

188

189

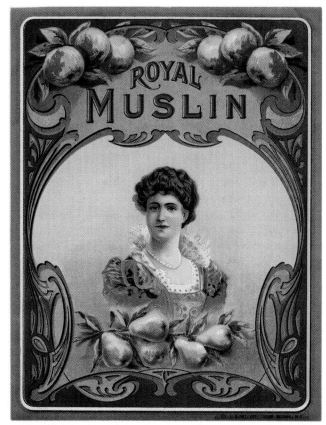

190

191

PICKLES

TRADE MARK

RED CABBAGE

192

BRAND

DISTRIBUTED BY
QUINCY
WHOLESALE GROCERY INC.
QUINCY, MASS.

193

LILY CHOCOLATES

Ganong Bros.
ST. STEPHEN, N.B.

194

Sirop
**citron
fantaisie**
pur sucre

195

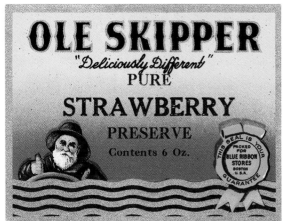

OLE SKIPPER
"Deliciously Different"
PURE
STRAWBERRY
PRESERVE
Contents 6 Oz.

THIS SEAL IS YOUR
PACKED FOR
BLUE RIBBON
STORES
BOSTON
U.S.A.
GUARANTEE

196

INDIA

CRESCENT TURMERIC

197

PAPRIKA·SPAIN

198

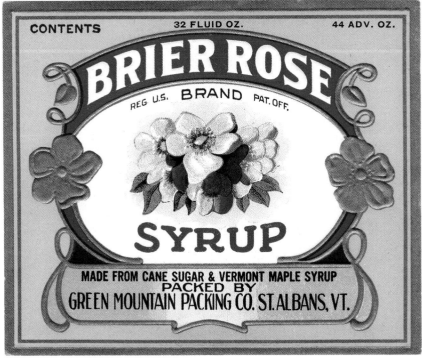

CONTENTS   32 FLUID OZ.   44 ADV. OZ.

BRIER ROSE
REG. U.S.   BRAND   PAT. OFF.

SYRUP

MADE FROM CANE SUGAR & VERMONT MAPLE SYRUP
PACKED BY
GREEN MOUNTAIN PACKING CO. ST. ALBANS, VT.

199

OLD COLONY
BRAND
CANE &   MAPLE
SYRUP
PREPARED FOR DISCRIMINATING TRADE,
BAY STATE MAPLE SYRUP CO.
BOSTON, MASS.

200

P.C.FLEIT & Co's
New Season's
Estd. P.C.F 1843. P.C.F. Co.
APPLE & GOOSEBERRY JAM
KIRKWALL.

201

KLOSTERGADE 2 AARHUS
KAFFE
AAGAARDS
KAFFE
ERSTATNING
Den kan De li'!

202

MT. PLEASANT
GOLDEN GINGER ALE
MANUFACTURED FROM THE FINEST INGREDIENTS AND PURE GINGER EXTRACT. AGED UNDER BOND.
MT. PLEASANT BOTTLING WKS.
SKOWHEGAN, ME.

203

J. B. DICKEY,
BIRCH BEER
NEWTON, KANSAS.

204

SNAIDER SYRUP CORP.
AMERICAN BRAND
CONTENTS   One Half Gallon
WHOLE CHERRIES
Contains cane sugar syrup, selected cherries, artificial color, preserved with 1/10 of 1% Benzoate of Soda and Sulphur Dioxide.
Manufactured by
SNAIDER SYRUP CORP.
389 Bushwick Avenue, Brooklyn 6, N.Y.

205

New England
VERMONT
MAPLE SAP SYRUP
100% PURE
NEW ENGLAND MAPLE SYRUP CO.
BOSTON, MASS.
CONTENTS   ½ PINT

206

ALEXANDER
THE BELT THAT RIM GRIPS

207

ROVER
8
AMSTERDAM BROOM CO.
AMSTERDAM, N.Y.
THIS LABEL IS THE EXCLUSIVE PROPERTY OF THE AMSTERDAM BROOM CO. AMSTERDAM, N.Y. INFRINGEMENTS ARE FORBIDDEN

209

ARDUCO COMMUNITY
HUDSON-GOLD
THE Champagne
OF APPLE JUICES
MADE AND CARBONATED BY OUR OWN PROCESS
ARDUCO COMMUNITY
ARTHURSBURG DUTCHESS COUNTY, N.Y. & NEW YORK CITY
WHERE EVER THE FINEST IS SERVED ARDUCO COMMUNITY PRODUCTS ARE FOUND
A PURE FRUIT PRODUCT OF THE HIGHEST QUALITY FOR THE DISCRIMINATING
CONTENTS 12 FLD. OZ.

208

210

211

212

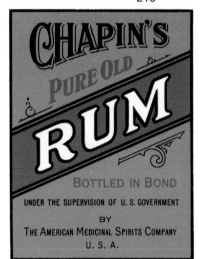

213

215

216

214

217

218

219

220

222

223

221

224

225

226

227

228

229

24   MISCELLANEOUS